PEREZ ON SPORTS

THE WHIMSICAL ART OF
JOSE S. PEREZ

WRS
PUBLISHING

A Division of WRS Group, Inc.
Waco, Texas

First published in the United States of America in 1996
by WRS Publishing, A Division of WRS Group, Inc.,
701 N. New Road, Waco, Texas 76710.
Book design by Kenneth Turbeville.
Jacket design by Joe James.

Printed in Hong Kong

10 9 8 7 6 5 4 3 2 1

Library of Congress Cataloging-in-Publication Data

Perez, Jose S., 1929-
    Perez on sports / Jose S. Perez.
        p.   cm.
    ISBN 1-56796-125-8
    1. Sports--Caricatures and cartoons. 2. American wit and humor,
Pictorial.   I. Title.
NC1429.P3967A4   1995
741.5'973--dc20
                                                    95-22517
                                                        CIP

DEDICATION

*T*his book is dedicated to athletes and fans of all sports, including many I have not been able to illustrate. In doing these paintings, many times I relied upon my own experiences as a youngster when I played basketball, volleyball, and other games at which, for lack of skill, I was a complete failure for reference. I was a mess; sometimes I had a twisted finger or bruises all over my body. Luckily for me, my career in sports was short-lived, and at age 18 I quit those diversions and went to work.

I love and admire those who perform great feats in sports. I bow to these men and women for their eternal struggle for excellence as they go beyond normal human endurance to win medals, fame and glory, and to set new records. I pay no attention to their race, country, or flag. To me they are all equal entities from the planet Earth who share their talents with the rest of us.

I gratefully acknowledge my friend and patron, Dr. Wayman Spence, who has encouraged me and made this series of paintings and this book possible. I also thank Kenneth Turbeville, the design artist for my books, and Joe James for his talented cover designs. I thank Pam Schreiber, my editor, and lastly, I thank my wife, Mary, for years of support and love.

*J*ose *P*erez

TABLE OF CONTENTS

FOREWORD

In spite of our gross commercialization of athletics, and quotes, or misquotes, from Vince Lombardi, Leo Durocher and thousands of other coaches throughout history, sports are really not war. They are play, and play–unlike war–is something that at the time one is doing it is the most important thing in the world, but five minutes later is completely unimportant. Perez's paintings capture the play in sports like no other artist has ever done.

Perez, who will be counted as one of the foremost satirical painters in history, mixes human with anthropomorphic perspectives and scenes from medieval days to contemporary times in a way that is his own special trademark. Students of art and sports history should compare his paintings and drawings with the great artists of the past whose good-natured humor, and sometimes savage ridicule, satirized society in unforgettable ways. Boilly, Cruikshank, Daumier, Gillray, Hogarth, Kley and Rowlandson can all be seen in the canvases of Perez's work. But Perez has something extra special compared to these famous names found in prestigious museums. Perez is a contemporary American who mixes Mexican and American cultures, good times and bad times, foolishness and sincerity, talent and practice, and humility and pride.

As a publisher and art collector, nothing has given me more pleasure than working with and collecting the paintings of Jose Perez. He is as intriguing in person as his images are on canvas. Enjoy his wonderful paintings, and look for both obvious and subtly camouflaged meanings. This work represents the eyes, the heart and the soul of one of the greatest satirical artists to ever flip a brush at society.

Wayman R. Spence, M.D.

INTRODUCING JOSE PEREZ

With a personality as unique as his art, Jose Perez has painted his way through life. His paintings are his voice, his method of expressing himself, his commentary on society.

Born in Houston, Texas, on June 30, 1929, of Mexican parents, Perez moved with his family to Mexico when he was five years old. Returning to the United States as a teenager, Perez swam across the border carrying his papers which proved he was a U.S. citizen. His brother, also a U.S. citizen, had lost his papers and so talked Jose into swimming back to their country. This incident is a foreshadowing of the personality Perez was to become.

Jose developed a sense of humor in his early years, and it's been an integral part of his life and his art ever since. Through years of working in menial jobs, through his struggle for recognition as an artist, through a bout with glaucoma — through all the trying times of his life, Jose Perez has maintained his sense of humor.

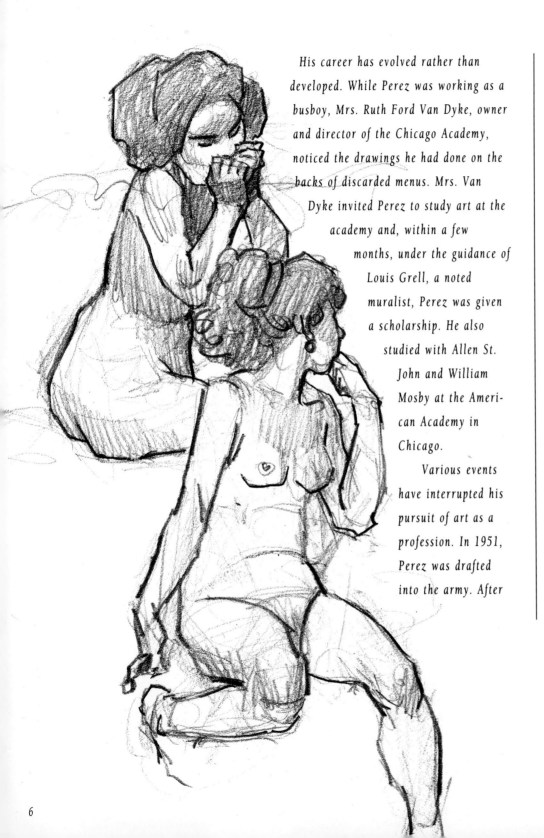

His career has evolved rather than developed. While Perez was working as a busboy, Mrs. Ruth Ford Van Dyke, owner and director of the Chicago Academy, noticed the drawings he had done on the backs of discarded menus. Mrs. Van Dyke invited Perez to study art at the academy and, within a few months, under the guidance of Louis Grell, a noted muralist, Perez was given a scholarship. He also studied with Allen St. John and William Mosby at the American Academy in Chicago.

Various events have interrupted his pursuit of art as a profession. In 1951, Perez was drafted into the army. After serving two years, he returned to the American Academy and studied art for another two years. He spent the next few years drifting from place to place, working at odd jobs — as a strawberry picker in Oregon, a construction worker in Houston, and a factory handyman in Chicago. Then, in 1958, he wandered to Washington, D.C., where he found the art ambience stimulating and where he started to paint professionally. His first art commission was to paint a series of large paintings depicting the American Revolution for the Drummer Boy Museum in Cape Cod, Massachusetts.

The confusion Perez had felt in earlier years evaporated when he began to concentrate on satirical art and pursue his profession seriously. His work is owned by a wide variety of art collectors in the United States and Europe, and in 1981, Houston, Texas declared a Jose S. Perez Day for its distinguished native artist.

In 1994, an exhibit at The National Library of Medicine of 28 Perez paintings on medicine received more attention than any other art exhibit in their history. CNN Television featured the exhibit worldwide, and The Wellcome Institute for the History of Medicine, London, said "Perez is a genius."

Perez says of his own work: "Satirical painting suits my needs as an artist: The freedom to distort and yet remain in the spectrum of the fine arts. It is also my best way to communicate with my fellow man. The social comment, in which satirical art expresses its power, is without malice; it merely represents my personal view of the world as I see it, either from a historical point, the present, or the future."

PEREZ

OLYMPICS OPENING CEREMONY

Supposedly Olympic sports are nonpolitical and noncommercial, but unfortunately nothing has been more political than the Olympics. Hitler's snub of Jesse Owens, Munich's massacre, Mexico City's raised fists, Russia's boycott, America's boycott, America's dream team's logo pout ... it never seems to end. Yet after all the posturing and manipulating, every four years the world's conflicts and despairs do seem to slow down just a little bit as we all turn our attention to the olympiads.

Sumptuous displays of balloons, music, fireworks and costumes open each Olympics, while television rights and audiences make billions for promoters. But in his art, Perez shows no recognizable flags, countries, heroes, shoe logos, or commercials. He believes that all Olympic competitors should be equal winners and amateurs at heart. His portrayal of the Olympic flame as a candle adds a sentimental, common touch and his parade platform is a tribute to his inexhaustible imagination.

Olympics Opening Ceremony – 48" x 96" (123cm x 246cm)

# BASEBALL

*J*ust as in the real game, there's no doubt who the star is in this painting. But from the looks of the hurler on the mound, who would ever guess that he's a multimillionaire with all the privileges of the rich and famous.

The cocky batter whose center of gravity leans perilously into the strike zone dares the pitcher to get a fastball by him. The plate ump hides behind the gorilla catcher, who plays with no protective gear and is obviously the toughest guy on the diamond.

How many photos can be taken of the moment of truth as ball meets bat? The answer seems to be — never enough. Meanwhile, in the stands behind home plate, there's no fear of foul tips, only relaxed enjoyment of the whole scene. Who would have thought when baseball was first played at Cooperstown in 1839, that it would become a worldwide sport, and an Olympic one at that?

The delightful little rabbits who almost steal the scene represent all the kids that used to watch minor league games in the good old days, through knotholes in the fences or by sneaking into the park under and over the boards.

Finally, guess what all those pockmarks are in the infield grass. They're probably spots where tobacco juice has rendered biological life impossible. I wonder what it's doing to the mouth of our pitcher?

*B*aseball – 24" x 30" (61.5cm x 77cm)

BASKETBALL

While most people think of basketball as a game of giants played in an endlessly long season on TV, the game owes its real soul to the millions of driveways, playgrounds and small-town gyms where regularly guys play.

Perez's mad rebound scramble looks a little like a rugby scrim, but the ball floating above the mass of outstretched arms lifts the eye upward, unlike the down and dirty direction of rugby.

Every time one examines this painting a new, interesting character seems to emerge. Notice the poor guy on the bottom of the pile with the ankle wrap all undone. The blasé kid sitting in front of number 0 is managing to stay cool no matter what, and number 28 shows that some white guys _can_ jump, although this player's vertical leap is probably about six inches.

Every player from the YMCA to the pros has all sorts of mixed emotions about spectators, whose personalities range from assassins to mothers. These Jekyll-and-Hyde vicarious participants in the game have become as important to television as the players themselves. Spike Lee and Jack Nicholson must be somewhere in this crowd.

Finally, the great Larry Bird would surely feel an affinity with the bird flying toward the ball. But what in the world is a nest doing in Perez's basket? Maybe he's just trying to say that these guys are such poor shots there's not much need to keep it clean.

*B*asketball – 24" x 30" (61.5cm x 77cm)

OXING

It's hard to figure out where the best fight is in this arena — in the ring or in the stands. The white-clad referee takes one's eye first to the ring where the bloodied and beaten fighter in the blue trunks is being declared the winner, while the poor loser in the red trunks, fresh and unscathed, dubiously accepts the judge's bewildering decision like so many other political losers in olympics past. And from the looks of things, the ring announcer had better get himself back into the safety of the ring, or those pugilistic fans gone crazy may kill him next.

The moral of this painting is to never leave your fate in the hands of judges susceptible to political influences — in the ring or out.

Boxing – 24" x 30" (61.5cm x 77cm)

CYCLING

The Tour de France may be the most publicized and glamorized bicycle race in the world, but Perez's cyclists exemplify a spirit that every race director would kill for.

The large tiger on the tricycle first draws the viewer's eye, but notice the spectator leopard at the left side of the canvas. As he holds his baby in his arms, next to the man holding his human baby, Perez presents a metaphor of the commonality of all species in the animal kingdom.

There are over 40 other characters in this scene, and each one can be examined over and over again because different insights come with each change in mood.

As the cyclists near the finish line, a unicyclist and a tricyclist are in the lead, but leads easily vanish and the striped cyclist who has been drafting till the last moment will in all probability swing past them to win the prize.

Perez is an active defender of our environment, and also makes a statement for the nonpolluting nature of bicycling as he shows the countryside with crystal clear air.

Cycling – 24" x 30" (61.5cm x 77cm)

 **IVING**

Diving brings out the child in all of us, and Perez's characters remind us of the great times we had as kids doing all sorts of crazy dives just to show off. In many ways, in spite of all the commercialization, the Olympics and all their grandeur are actually not very far removed from the spirit of this painting.

The hippo has just scored a 9.8 with his bellybuster dive that will almost empty the pool and soak the spectators. The look in the eyes of the alligator tells us that he can't wait to do his thing, if there's any water left. Will the rhino cleanly break the water surface with his horn, and will the Chinese girl dive alone or on his shoulders? Why is the lion clutching the ball, and can you imagine the triple somersaults the two baboons are planning? Standing below the lion and behind the baboon, the cheetah-like character pointing at the diver probably has the best body composition for this sport. The underdog tiger, with the tire around his middle, standing at the foot of the diving tower is everyone's favorite.

Diving – 24" x 30" (61.5cm x 77cm)

EQUESTRIAN

Maybe it's because the best athletes in this sport are the horses, not the humans, but the EQUESTRIAN shows just how much fun the Olympics, and all sports, should be. After all, it's supposed to be the Olympic games, not the Olympic wars.

Perez says this whole event is Greek to him, and depicts two popular Greek mythological figures – Centaur and Pegasus – engaged in a race in which the former is more preoccupied with his personal love life than his desire to win the contest. Pegasus is more confident, almost arrogant, for he seems assured of victory as he easily flies over the obstacles. The other contenders, mere mortals, don't stand a chance because their performances are never perfect.

The spectators are, as often happens, more concerned with the quality of wine and political issues than the drama of the race. Besides, they know who's going to win – Pegasus! He does it every time.

*E*questrian – 24" x 30" (61.5cm x 77cm)

 IGURE SKATING

Everyone knows that big-boned, wide-hipped endomorphs simply can't compete with small-boned, aesthetically sculptured ectomorphs when it comes to the most graceful of all Olympic sports — figure skating. But, while figure skaters represent a genetically-endowed combination of sex appeal and athleticism, by virtue of television the sport has created millions of out-of-shape fantasy skaters who can be just as graceful in their dreams as their beautiful Olympic heroes.

The handsome couple in the middle of Perez's ice rink are as graceful as they are large. Twirling and gliding over the ice like weightless astronauts, there is no doubt in anyone's mind that they are Olympic winners. They are making history and will be the talk of the sport for years to come. The Walter Mitty in all of us cheers for these big phenotypes while we publicly adore the thin, wistful figures we can never be.

Figure Skating – 24" x 30" (61.5cm x 77cm)

FOOTBALL

American football certainly can be accused of being a violent game, and all the metaphors from bombs to blitzes support this allegation. But Perez says that football is first and foremost a big boy's way of playing king-of-the-mountain.

In this painting, the elephant backfield has done its work — the football has crossed the goal line and the medieval cheerleaders have begun their touchdown dance. The faceless fans in the stands can now cheer or groan, depending on which side they sit. How can anyone look at this playful scene and not imagine football in the Olympics?

The 1932 Summer Olympics in Los Angeles featured 1,328 athletes from 37 countries competing in 128 events. The 1996 Summer Games in Atlanta, Georgia will host approximately 11,000 athletes from 196 countries competing for medals in 271 events. There will be room for football. And when it happens, can you imagine what a USA dream team made up of future Joe Montanas and Jerry Rices will do to teams from Chile and Portugal? 400-0 might be a close game.

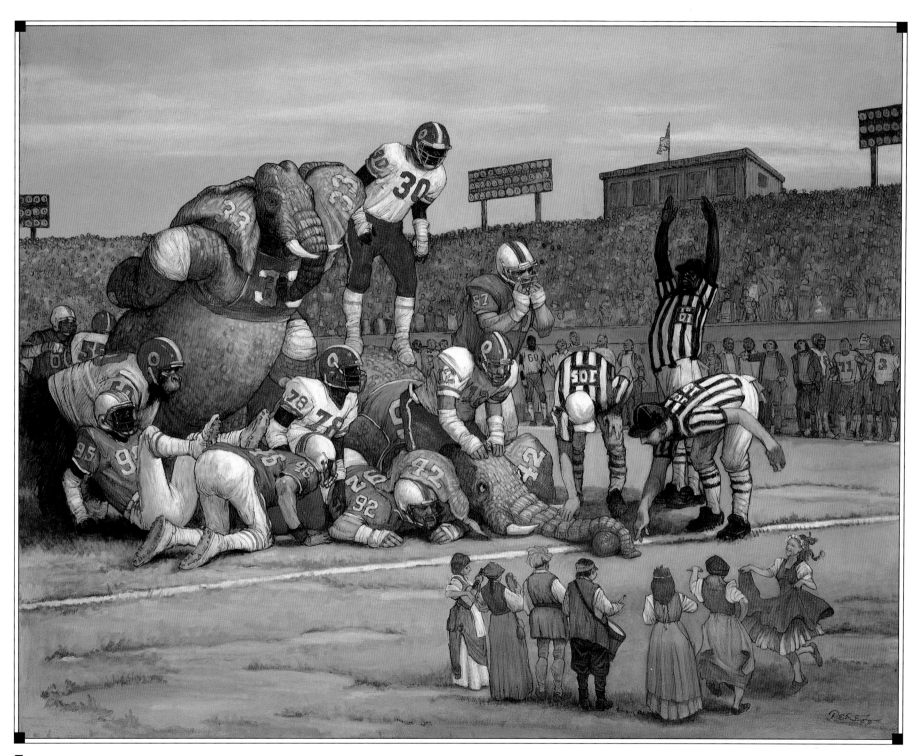

*F*ootball – 24" x 30" (61.5cm x 77cm)

OLF

This painting should charm the pants off of any golfer. Perez has depicted an unlikely accident: a golf ball has struck an innocent rabbit. In keeping with the spirit of our politically correct times, a protest is being staged by all the natural inhabitants of the golf course. As the elected spokesman reads the charges brought against the golfers, accusing them of violating animal rights, the body language of the golfers ranges from defiance to a little bit ashamed.

Perez is a great lover of animals, and suggests that golf courses should adopt different rules for different times. Golfers play during the day, and the critters use the course at night.

While golf is one of the few worldwide sports not yet credited with Olympic status, surely it will join the group. If boxing with all of its brutality and judging scandals, modern pentathlon which is neither modern nor telegenic, synchronized swimming which is little more than shipwreck ballet, and rhythmic gymnastics, where an inadvertent exposure of a bra strap means automatic point deduction, can be Olympic sports, then golf with all of its heritage, dignity and television appeal will certainly someday grace the events.

Golf – 24" x 30" (61.5cm x 77cm)

GYMNASTICS

No other Olympic sport reminds us of the natural-born antics of our evolutionary ancestors as much as gymnastics. Perez imagines that these creatures may have their own olympics, set among crystal-clear water ponds, lush ferns and giant tree branches. And in this case, the animals have invited humans to the competition.

This whimsical portrayal of an uncommercialized, nontelevised Olympics set deep in the forest needs no further written description. It is so natural and appealing, from the theatrical girl in the orangutan's palm to the two little girls sitting so innocently with the monkey. In freezing this moment of unstaged camaraderie, void of any mean, competitive spirits or fears of failure, Perez may have captured the way gymnastics should be better than any contemporary painter has done before.

Gymnastics – 24" x 30" (61.5cm x 77cm)

ICE HOCKEY

The hockey players are ready for one very big collision as they converge on the puck. Everyone knows a fight will break out and sticks will fly. Can you imagine the body block the hippo will put on the bear? Since circus bears have been trained to wrestle and roller skate, maybe a trained bear could actually play hockey. The penguins and birds, passive spectators for the moment, watch until the big bang moment when they'll surely come out of their seats.

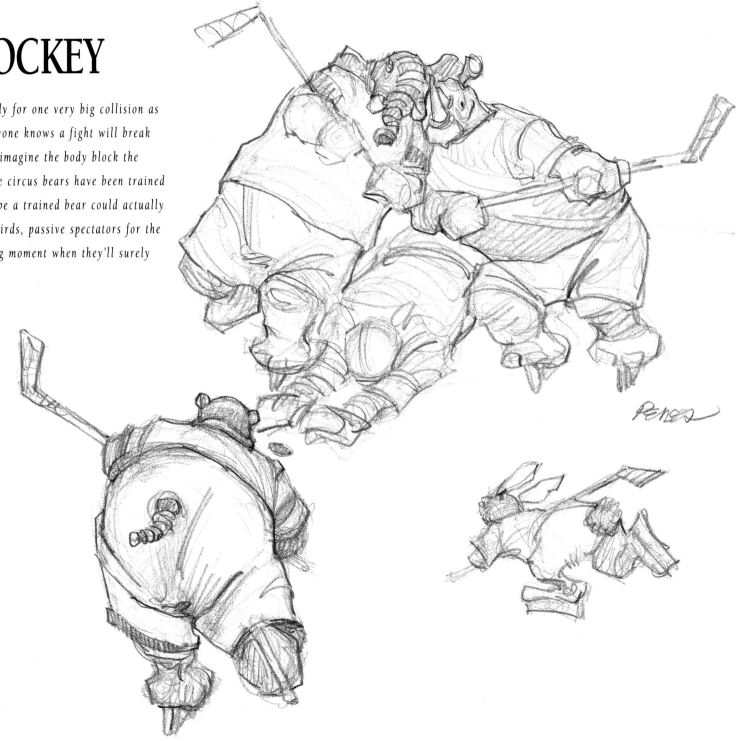

Ice Hockey – 24" x 30" (61.5cm x 77cm)

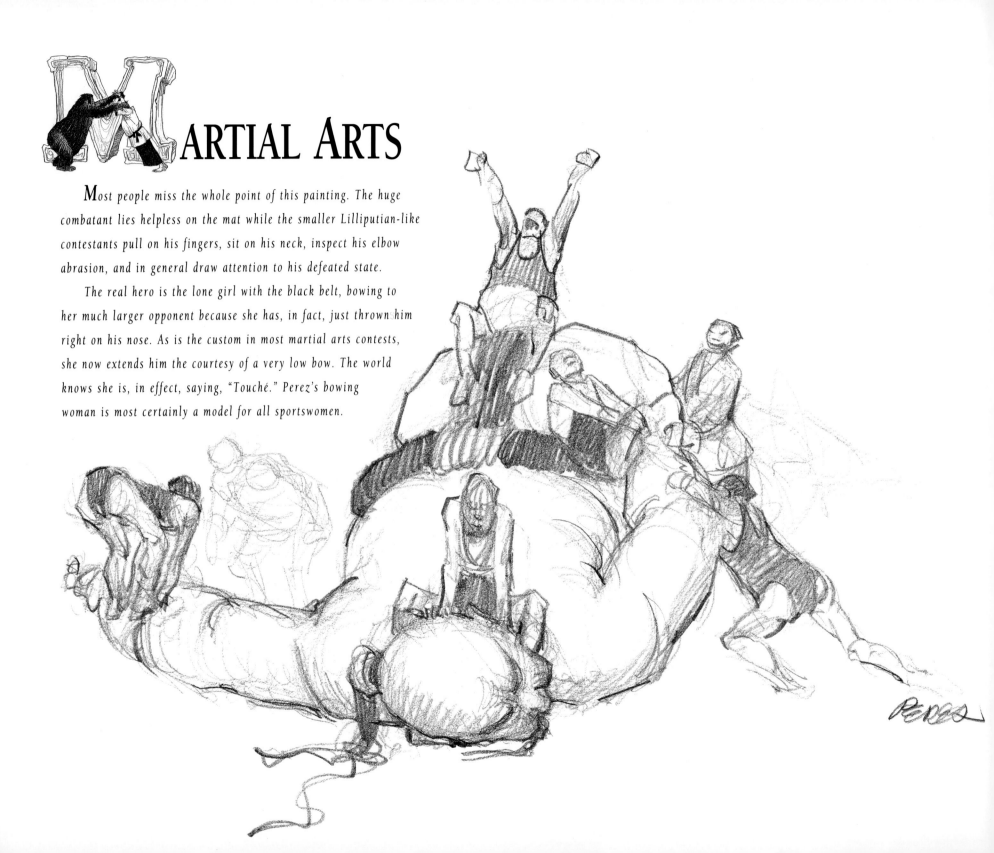

MARTIAL ARTS

Most people miss the whole point of this painting. The huge combatant lies helpless on the mat while the smaller Lilliputian-like contestants pull on his fingers, sit on his neck, inspect his elbow abrasion, and in general draw attention to his defeated state.

The real hero is the lone girl with the black belt, bowing to her much larger opponent because she has, in fact, just thrown him right on his nose. As is the custom in most martial arts contests, she now extends him the courtesy of a very low bow. The world knows she is, in effect, saying, "Touché." Perez's bowing woman is most certainly a model for all sportswomen.

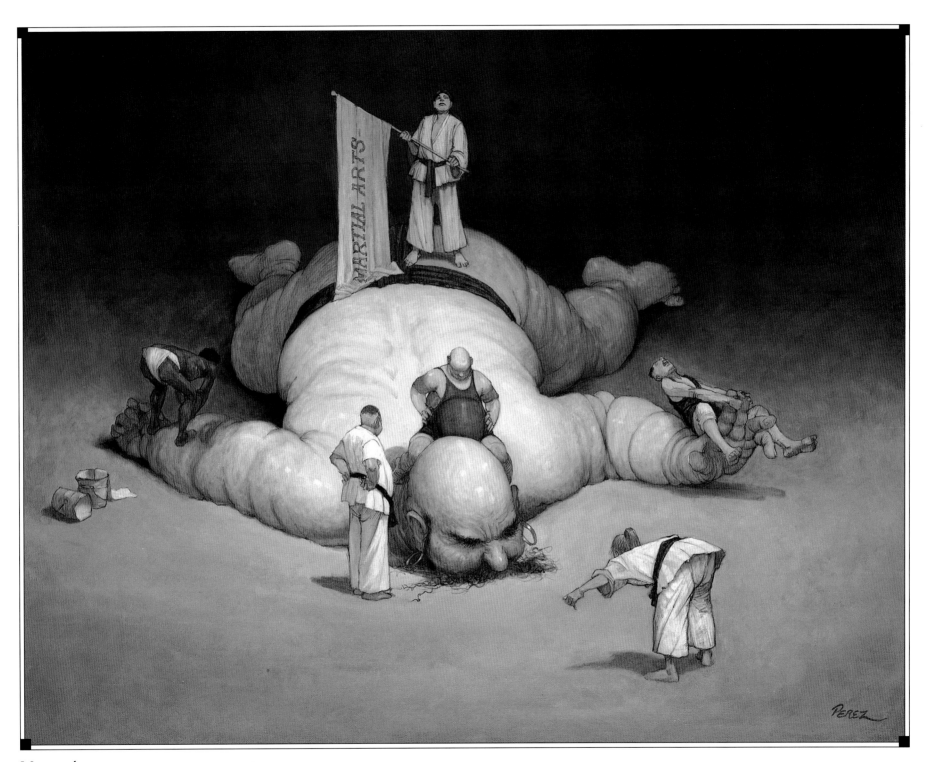

Martial Arts – 24" x 30" (61.5cm x 77cm)

# ROWING

Perez says that during the course of this painting he could hear music and the sounds of a symphonette ringing in his ears. He felt this must have been the way it was in the old days of rowing competitions, when the higher the waves the louder the coxswain had to holler.

The lone surfer is about to be overrun, or is he? Maybe his agile, lightweight craft will ride the wave all the way to the finish line, ahead of the big boys.

*R*owing – 24" x 30" (61.5cm x 77cm)

# SKIING

Look out! Here comes the overweight, out-of-shape, out-of-control, middle-aged flat lander who hits the slopes once a year and scares the mountain natives half to death. The two chaps standing side by side have seen it all before, and know there is no use in even trying to give this skier any advice because he won't listen anyway. At least three other skiers have gone down in his tracks, and the rabbit running for his life may or may not make it to safety. The penguins are unperturbed because they have enough sense to stay off the slopes when flat landers are on a skiing vacation.

Skiing – 24" x 30" (61.5cm x 77cm)

SOCCER

Perez's painting tells a delightful fairy tale about the world's favorite game of football.

The day began with a gloomy, gray sky, followed by westerly winds howling like banshees in agony. Later, fat, dark clouds rolled in, adding to the dreadfulness of the afternoon. Just as the rain was ready to roll and it appeared things could not have gotten any worse, they did.

This was the day in history when the sports' committee decided to ban all rhinoceroses from playing the game of soccer, because of the damage they cause when heading the ball. Perez captures the moment when the head of the delegation is about to deliver his speech.

The drummer has announced the arrival of the committee, and is perhaps a metaphor of a lawyer's letter warning of an impending investigation by the Amateur Athletic Union. The sad-faced rhino, with the ball stuck on his horn, really doesn't know what to do. His teammates and opposing players are all solemn and sympathetic, some even crying. The spectators at the top of the soccer net have no encouragement to add, and it seems like a very sad day for fair play.

Soccer – 24" x 30" (61.5cm x 77cm)

SOFTBALL

Softball is the fastest growing adult team sport in America. While it hasn't yet received the honor of being selected as an Olympic sport, its day will come. After all, cricket, croquet and tug-of-war have been included in modern Olympics,

Women's softball is the subject of this painting and Perez's circling, cheering, crazy, conglomeration of fans gives the sport its own personality. In contrast to Perez's baseball painting, there is no evidence of tobacco spitting, cursing or fighting by the women. And while a prolonged theatrical tantrum would likely follow this ump's call if these were men players, the girl in red will undoubtedly accept the close call without a bit of grandstanding temper.

Softball – 24" x 30" (61.5cm x 77cm)

SWIMMING

As Neptune raises his hand, he points with his index finger toward the sky, a sign that he is ready to let go of the thunderbolt which will start the fastest of the swimming events — the freestyle race.

The body language of the contestants tells a story of readiness and comic suspense, and their conglomerate swimming styles certainly fit a freestyle definition. Who knows who the favorite should be — the octopus, the female in blue, the stretching male, the big-tusked one, the woman in the green bikini, the character straddling the penguin waiting to be pulled by a shark, the other penguin, the alligator, or the mermaid? What an eclectic collection of swimmers!

Swimming – 24" x 30" (61.5cm x 77cm)

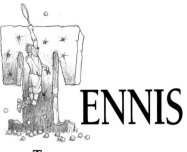

TENNIS

The real fun in watching tennis is at court side, where one can hear the bangs of the ball, feel the grunts from the players, and watch their between-point antics. Television may offer close-ups, but it loses the visceral parts of the game.

Because this is mixed doubles, there's no big crowd and no TV cameras. Like any typical club match, the males are trying to dominate and show their toughness. But the women control themselves and are not the least intimidated.

This scene is filled with numerous stereotypes from the bored, sleeping netsman to the military stances of the ball boys. The crowd has an international flavor and, unlike tennis crowds of years past, is openly enthusiastic as it enjoys cheering for its favorite. While the action on center court takes one's eye at first, the emotional scene is stolen by the little girl at the lemonade stand. Somehow one knows that she'll be a star herself someday.

Tennis – 30" x 24" (77cm x 61.5cm)

TRACK

Every character in this race deserves the eyes' undivided attention, but like a real race, one's tendency is to lose the personality of each runner in the mass of the pack.

The tortoise appears to be in the lead, and the court attendant's sign says they're about to begin the final lap. Has the poor tortoise been lapped, or is he really beating the hare again?

Who is the centaur carrying in his arms, and who is the poor, courageous fellow with the blue toga personifying as he tries to crawl his way to the finish line? Real marathoners have on occasion looked as fatigued.

Notice the racer in the football suit. He apparently can't wait to turn pro. What about the ostrich coming up on the left of the rhinoceros? It's anybody's guess who will win Perez's race.

The rabbits are naturally cheering for their own species, while the rest of the spectators seem pretty impartial, except for the two Greeks at the top left who may get rather nasty if their favorite doesn't win. All in all, this menagerie of spectators is amazingly like the cross section seen at any club road race.

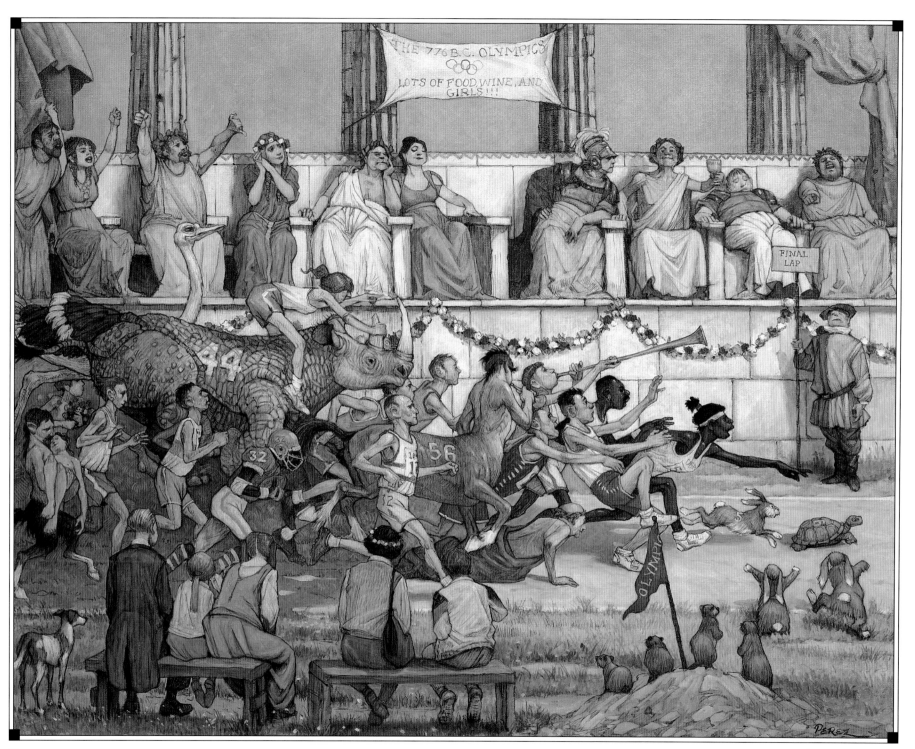

Track – 24" x 30" (61.5cm x 77cm)

TRACK AND FIELD

While Perez has filled his Olympics with countless imaginative characters, none can top these contestants.

The gargantuan hammer-thrower, who in keeping with the history of this event is no kid, dominates the infield, but the panda bear with the garbage-can lid discus is about to steal the scene. No matter how far men can broad jump, either the cheetah or kangaroo will surely win the gold. Meanwhile, the pole vaulter, javelin-thrower, high-jumper, and female shot-putter can easily be overlooked by a cursory glance. The candle on the Olympic rings is a final aesthetic touch to this most whimsical of all the Perez paintings.

Track and Field – 24" x 30" (61.5cm x 77cm)

 # VOLLEYBALL

Who but Perez would ever think of staging a
volleyball game on the deck of a pirate ship?

This painting came from Perez's imaginative
flashback to the time he played volleyball in the fifth
grade. He dreaded those balls flying across the net
like missiles being fired from a cannon straight at
him. He still remembers how much it hurt trying
to tip the ball with his fingers, and hasn't
forgotten the pain of a sprained thumb or
the burn of a spanked palm.

The halter-clad girl with the bare midriff spiking the
ball reminds one of today's beach volleyball, which is
indeed an Olympic sport on its own for the 1996 Games.
In these days of political correctness, beach volleyball
offers equal opportunity viewing, as both men and women
compete in skimpy bathing suits.

*V*olleyball – 24" x 30" (61.5cm x 77cm)

WEIGHTLIFTING

This wonderful painting defies a simple interpretation; it is perhaps the most psychoanalytical of any of Perez's sports art. One can study the work for hours and still discover a figure, expression or prop completely overlooked before.

Perez says ancient myths concerning Atlas holding up the world led him to this surrealistic expression of a weight lifter trying to military press a barbell weighted with elephants and rhinoceroses on one side and a group of people on the other. Notice the barbell is leaning to the human side, which outweighs even the largest of animals.

Study the expressions of the various spectators. They're not actually exaggerated at all. The real spectators at a weight-lifting competition are every bit as much fun to watch as the lifters themselves.

Perez's sense of anatomy is absolutely exquisite in his treatment of the lifter, from his red knees to his mammoth, arched posture. Perhaps if the lifter can pause long enough, with the barbell resting on his chest and shoulders, a few more human weights will fall off and he'll be able to hoist this preposterous weight above his head.

W*eightlifting* – 30" x 24" *(77cm x 61.5cm)*

WRESTLING

Who but Perez would ever have thought of portraying the oldest sport in the world by setting the scene at the bottom of the ocean with a heavyweight grappler going up against an octopus? But after thinking about it for a while, the metaphor is perfect because many wrestling opponents seem like all arms and legs.

Unlike the ludicrous sport of professional wrestling, Olympic freestyle and Greco-Roman wrestling are strictly legit, and Perez's wrestlers are obviously giving it all they've got.

As important as the wrestlers are themselves, the menagerie of spectators really make this painting. The two benches, each wildly cheering for their favorite wrestler, remind one of mat maids in a high school wrestling match. The sharks make one think of other wrestlers watching a match and just dying to get onto the mat themselves. The walrus sitting by himself is like an old coach remembering every second of his own matches forty years ago.

Notice the sea horses — perfect representatives of quick, little light-weights watching big, slow heavyweights plodding through a match. Meanwhile the fish all have their eyes glued on the competition. Viva la wrestling–the oldest sport in the world.

*W*restling – 24" x 30" (61.5cm x 77cm)

SPORTS MEDICINE

A gargantuan figure, the doctor in this painting sits on his
unique throne of bones and conveys a sense of power and authority.
The ruins of the Roman wall and the Egyptian nurse standing in front
of the doctor are signs that orthopedics is one of the oldest branches
of medicine. In fact, archaeologists and paleontologists have found
evidence of set bones dating back to primitive times.

Various athletes approach the doctor's throne to ask in
reverential fashion for healing of their sports injuries. They
probably know that complete obedience to the doctor's
commands will be demanded of them. The doctor will surely
tell them to stop doing whatever they are doing, or, if they're
not doing something, to begin it.

The enormous size accorded the doctor could reflect the fact
that many orthopedists played football in their college days and
still enjoy being on the sidelines in their role as physicians.
Or it could simply be acknowledgment of the degree of
trust placed in him by his patients, who are
probably the most compliant of patients
because of their desire to return to their
sport as soon as possible.

Sports Medicine – 24" x 30" (61.5cm x 77cm)

61